An Executive Personal Development Series

The Curses of a Thousand Mothers

How we Pursue Joyful Sins

Thejendra Sreenivas

Book Publishing Coach

www.thejendra.com

Table of Contents

About the Series

The **Executive Personal Development Series** is a set of short non-fiction books on business management, leadership, inspirational, motivational, and self-improvement topics. Each book is an imaginary discussion between a retired professor who thinks unconventionally and a corporate executive who thinks like the crowd. This is a unique professor who thinks, "*What is popular may not be right, and what is right may not be popular.*"

Most self-help books are normally written in a textbook or step-by-step guide formats. But these books are written like a novel in a conversational style with interactive lectures, candid arguments, and idle talk between the two who belong to different generations. Each book discusses some self-improvement concept or an aspect of the executive's personal or professional life and the professor enlightens, alters, or completely demolishes the executive's earlier thinking and assumptions.

The first book in the series is **The Power of**

Laziness followed by **The Extreme Minimalist** and others. However, each book can be read independently.

Preface

"Hey, have you committed any sins today?"

"No."

"No? How about yesterday?"

"No."

"No? What about the day before yesterday?"

"Hey, stop asking stupid questions! I am no sinner."

"Oh, come on, tell me the truth. How many sins did you collect today?"

"Now stop accusing me, okay? What sort of silly discussion is this? I said I am no sinner."

"Are you sure?"

"Yes, I am damn sure!"

"But how are you damn sure?"

"Look, I pay my taxes, I am a law-abiding citizen, I haven't killed anybody, and I give the best to my family, and hence I am no sinner! Stop asking rubbish questions. Besides, I don't believe in such ancient crap."

"But why don't you believe in it?"

"Hey, it is the 21st century, stupid! Concepts like sins are just superstitious garbage. It is pure nonsense, idiotic, lies, hogwash, foolish, silly, brainless, humbug, bullshit, irrational, crazy, absurd, ridiculous, stupid, and gobbledygook, believed only by spiritual lunatics who have lost the plot! I laugh and sneer at such trash!"

"Hmm, okay. I loved your maniacal laugh. So, what sins have you committed today?"

"Hey, are you on rewind or something? Didn't you understand what I said? I told you I am no sinner."

A Few Good Sins

After completing many interesting workshops, my visits to the professor became sporadic. Besides, my office work, the cold winter, and business travel kept me busy. Yet, I had not forgotten him. But it had been nearly three months since I saw the professor or called him for some advice. So, I dropped by his office to say hello.

"Hello! Look who is here on a nice Sunday. Where were you all these days, my dear chap?"

"Oh, I was busy with many things, professor. So, how are things?"

"Fine, even I was quite busy. I now have plenty of students all recommended by you."

"Yeah, I had told them about your unique workshops, and they got interested."

Suddenly, I got a phone call, excused myself, and went to the next room to talk. After I finished my call, the professor asked,

"Who was it?"

"It was from my TV repair company. It was the customer service manager."

"Why were you shouting at him?"

"Well, my new TV had broken down, and they promised to send a repairman at 6 pm yesterday. But that fellow came at 8 pm and wasted my two hours. So, I complained to their customer cell. This was a follow-up call, and I gave them some fireworks."

"Did they not repair the TV?"

"They did."

"Then why did you complain?"

"Well, that repair fellow came two hours late, professor. This is why I complained."

"What's the big deal with a couple of hours? Maybe he got stuck somewhere. Besides, it's a miserable winter now."

"That's not acceptable, professor. They need to honor their commitments."

The professor's face became a bit serious and said,

"You shouldn't be doing such sinful activities, my young chap."

"Sinful? Hey, professor, are you turning spiritual? What's sinful about my complaint?"

"You put the repairman in trouble over a trivial delay of two hours, didn't you?"

"But they should stick to their committed time, professor. It's the first law of customer satisfaction."

"Maybe, but I still say what you did was wrong. There was no need to complain against him when he did repair the TV but got slightly delayed."

"But customers nowadays are very demanding, professor. They don't tolerate nonsense or delays from any service providers."

"Let them be demanding. Why should you follow that stupid herd?"

"I don't understand your argument, professor. What's wrong or sinful about what I did?"

"I have a personal theory about how we pursue joyful sins. Would you be interested to listen?"

"Joyful sins? What happened to you, professor? Are you turning spiritual?"

"Well, I have always been spiritual. That is also a self-improvement subject that I study and advise."

"Hmm, interesting. So, what is this joyful sin that you are talking about?"

"Let me start by first defining sin. A general dictionary defines sin in various ways, like the transgression of divine law, a willful or deliberate violation of some religious or moral principle, etc."

"Okay."

"And spiritual believers always claim that you will suffer in life or have no peace of mind if you commit any sins."

"That's typical ancient superstitious stuff, professor."

"Yes, that's what most people today say. They don't care or will be cynical about what the spiritual people preach. However, they confidently assume that if they mind their own business, are law-abiding, pay their taxes on time, give their family the best of everything, pursue a higher standard of living, cut costs, are tough demanding customers, don't injure or kill another human, etc., then they are automatically leading a clean sin-free life. Is this what you also think?"

"Yes, even I think so."

"But is it really true? Are you really sin-free? The answer is a big No. Everyone commits sins almost continuously, either knowingly or unknowingly. And many of the honest and law-abiding activities you do daily are actually gory sins."

"Gory sins? Stop kidding, professor."

"No, I am not kidding."

"But how is it possible? I don't understand what you are trying to say."

"You will. Just answer a few simple questions first."

"Do you like buying fancy gadgets like mobiles, music devices, computers, cars, etc.?"

"Yes. In fact, I have all the latest and greatest products."

"Do you demand the best from your service providers?"

"Yes. I am a very demanding customer. I tolerate no nonsense from any service providers."

"Do you own stocks in top companies?"

"Of course, I am a stockholder of plenty of top companies. And I own plenty of cool stuff those companies manufacture."

"Do you like watching movies about real wars, crime stories, etc.?"

"Yes, I love them. In fact, I collect movies and books of all real stories."

"Do you love your family?"

"Yes, I give them the best!"

"Hmm, looks like you are already a great sinner. Congratulations!"

"Hey, how do those simple things make me a sinner, professor? It sounds ridiculous! My understanding of sin is I should indulge in killing, violence, and destruction of others to become a sinner. Right?"

"Wrong! You need not directly kill or injure anyone. But you can still become a great sinner just by continuing the simple, legitimate things you are currently doing."

"But how? I don't see the connection."

"There is a deep connection if you look a bit hard. But before we get to that, just look at some of the behaviors of modern customers today. There was a time when tolerance and moderation were normal, except for critical life-saving activities and things. Customers and competition did exist, but they did not have a ruthless killer instinct to get to the top regardless of the consequences. But today moderation and tolerance are going downhill.

Secondly, advertisers make you believe that if you don't have the latest and the greatest stuff you will be ridiculed by your friends, or you will lose your boyfriend or girlfriend, or you will lose your job, or you are a loser, and so on. Therefore, you must go and buy that latest and greatest electronic gadget, cosmetics, car, watch, suit, motorbike, or some other rubbish, or else you are a loser! And it is also highly fashionable and glamorous nowadays to be demanding and uncompromising. Customers today want everything right now, right here, and want new amazing stuff delivered faster and cheaper every few months. And ignorant folks like you will unconsciously get sucked into such false thinking and start acting like that because of the constant marketing bombardment."

"Hey, it's the 21st century, professor. Plenty of people are like that. Time is money. What's wrong with that?"

"Well, everything is wrong. You are not a winner, but a sinner!"

"I don't believe you, professor. You sound wacky."

"Now hold your surprise and outrage. You may be wondering how these seemingly innocent and legal activities like buying cool electronic gadgets, driving fancy cars, the latest computers, owning stocks, being a demanding customer, etc., can make you a sinner. Besides, you have bought those goodies with your hard-earned money and not by robbing anyone. Nevertheless, you may be surprised to know how most such activities aimed at a relentless pursuit of a higher and higher standard of living can actually make you a big sinner, directly or indirectly. Secondly, contrary to popular belief, sinners are not only those people who commit murders, indulge in violence, etc. Ordinary, law-abiding people can also become great sinners without being directly involved in committing any crime or spilling blood."

"But how is it possible, professor? This is how modern consumer markets work."

"I have a different theory. My theory of sin is based on a simple concept of how you can fall sick by eating a fish, which could have eaten some shit. That is, we can commit sins ourselves, or we can allow others to commit sins on our behalf. Secondly, evil deeds are not always caused by evil people just for the heck of it. You need to see who the driving force behind them is."

"Who is that driving force?"

"That driving force is the modern customers (like you and me) who unknowingly choose evil by mistaking it for happiness. It's the so-called good and innocent people who constantly coax and encourage tough people to do wicked things to satisfy your endless needs. And it is tough, demanding, and uncompromising customers like you who sponsor many organized crimes and mafias worldwide. Modern people can sleep peaceably in their beds at night only because rough men are ever ready to do violence on their behalf."

"I am fully confused now. Where is the connection between organized crime and what customers like me do?"

"To understand how, just look at the sources of your sin and how the various popular things you do are directly or indirectly sponsoring crime."

Source-1: Your love for expensive trinkets - Who doesn't love to own expensive things like gold, diamonds, precious gems, etc.? Romance stories are dripping with tales of how sissy boyfriends have sold their souls to buy diamonds and jewels for their girlfriends. But how many customers really know what goes on behind the glittering scenes? Gold, diamonds, and other precious stuff don't grow on trees. They are extracted from hot and deep mines through hard labor, working in unprintable conditions. But because certain stupid humans are willing to pay a king's ransom for these shiny, useless trinkets, gangsters commit hundreds of atrocities to make them easily available in the market. For example, a diamond could have been obtained through various criminal methods like murder, extortion, slave trade, harsh mining, etc., and you will never know about it. Nobody will tell you, and you don't care anyway. But you must have that diamond for your anniversary or birthday to see that gorgeous smile on your wife or girlfriend or hear them squeal with delight. Why care about how and where it was obtained?"

"Hmm, that makes some sense. What else?"

"Source-2: Your standard of living - Higher and higher standards of living also sponsor crime."

"How?"

"Customers love to own big houses, cars, electronics, phones, computers, wooden furniture, leather items, furs, perfumes, and other fancy stuff. So, industrialists and businessmen will plunder and ravage villages, forests, tribal lands, and agricultural land, use slave labor in factories, etc., to extract metals, minerals, sand, stones, animal skin, oil, wood, and other stuff required to manufacture such goods and pump them into the market. Similarly, every fancy thing that customers crave will indirectly result in the creation of various criminals who will commit assorted crimes ranging from child labor to mass murders to fulfill the never-ending consumer demands. And customers are unable or unwilling to care about behind-the-scenes crimes as long as they get happiness from the objects they desire."

"Hmm, that sounds bad."

Source-3: How you sponsor slave factories - Have you ever considered how our supermarkets and malls are filled with every conceivable gadget, or how newer and cheaper gadgets arrive on the shelves every week? You can see mountains and mountains of plastic and electronic goods, and almost all are non-biodegradable stuff. How do you think it is possible to buy a big TV set for just a hundred dollars, or a pair of shoes for fifteen dollars, or umpteen other goods for two dollars these days? For example, you can even throw away a TV set every month and buy a new one with your pocket money. Such low costs were not possible a few years ago. How is this possible now?"

"I am not sure, professor. Better cost control, I suppose."

"Not always. Terrible human costs are built into every cheap and fancy goodie you love to own. It's because of relentless greed and impatience by customers like you that companies now outsource inordinate amounts of their work to countries that don't have good labor laws. What's illegal in one country is a normal business practice in a poor country, and top international companies take advantage of that. They don't go to third-world countries to improve diplomatic and cultural relations. They go there because there are no proper labor rules and environmental controls that hinder their financial greed and customer cravings. So, what they do there is technically not illegal.

So, they turn a blind eye to inhumane working conditions and the exploitation of workers who slog long and hard in sweatshops and where hiring and firing happen without batting an eyelid. Companies push their employees to work faster and longer, cut corners, and make them work in dangerous conditions. Barbarians in suits negotiate with slave traders to get the kind of employees who will agree to work long hours for a pittance and exploit those workers to create stunning goods as cheaply as possible so that you can have the latest and greatest toy every day."

"Wow! Yes, I did read an article about how western companies outsource to cheap countries where they have terrible working conditions."

Source-4: How and where you invest - Investing money in various places for better returns may not seem like a crime. But how and where you invest also matters a lot. Behind every great fortune, there is always a hidden crime, even if they pay all taxes. Let us assume you own some stock of a reputed and profitable company giving you reasonably good returns. But are shareholders nowadays satisfied with anything? No, they are never pleased with the current profitability and steady growth. They want more and more money and astronomical growth week after week from the companies they invest in. So, what do they do? They gang up with other stockholders to grumble and pester the company management to do something in hostile shareholder meetings. The business media also goes berserk, accusing the company of losing direction, doubting its leadership, its future profitability, etc. And guess what will happen in a few days?"

"Not sure. What will the company do?"

"The company will immediately announce a major restructuring. And what does that usually mean? It means the CEO will announce a 15% cut in employees worldwide and plenty of other reckless cost-cutting and outsourcing measures to satisfy the gargantuan shareholder appetite, despite earning a healthy profit. The market quickly appreciates this bold move, and the stock starts zooming, and you start making more money than before. It is party time again! But behind the scenes is the creation of a slave factory somewhere, and you have also unnecessarily destroyed the livelihoods of thousands of employee families to get more money from the stock you own. Hence, shareholders and investors like you who applaud companies downsizing will now become sinners, as you will be making money out of someone's misery."

"Wow!"

"When people knowingly or unknowingly invest their money in companies that do evil, then such humans have to suffer for the sins committed by the business owners. If you are a beneficiary of crime money, directly or indirectly, then various sins will cling to you. Such sin money can bite you in uncanny ways. For example, you may invest your money in a company that is secretly and ruthlessly destroying forests and the livelihoods of tribes, villagers, natives, etc., to extract minerals. Or they could be manufacturing and selling weapons that are used by criminals and warmongers, and so on. Or you may invest in stocks of a booze or cigarette company, which will be destroying thousands of families. In other words, you could be knowingly or unknowingly sponsoring the harassment and untold misery of your fellow humans somewhere on the planet just by buying and promoting stocks of such companies. So, their sins will also cling to you because you are knowingly or unknowingly promoting their crimes."

"You are beginning to make great sense, professor."

"Economy is not more paramount than humanity. We can also consider other types of indirect examples."

"What are they?"

"For example, film producers make gripping films and documentaries on famous terrorism, crimes, murders, world wars, plane crashes, ships sinking, etc., by re-enacting those gory scenes to shock the audience and make tons of money in ticket sales and also get glittering awards from badly dressed celebrities.

Customers love oil so badly that they will lose all sanity over it. Because of this, governments and businessmen will easily create new enemies to wage wars and commit horrendous atrocities to get that oil from the ground so that customers can zoom around in their flashy cars.

Democratic countries that boast of great human rights easily support and ignore dictators, psychopaths, and authoritarian regimes if there are economic advantages in doing business with them.

Employees of the arms industry help mercenaries and warmongers create mayhem worldwide by inventing newer and better weapons that can quickly kill thousands of humans. And they also have annual weapons exhibitions where warmongers come and drool at the latest stunning fighter planes and other shiny weapons that can wipe out a city in minutes. All these people have invisible bloodstains on their hands."

"Amazing connection, professor."

"The list can go on and on. And all modern customers are directly or indirectly benefitting from such atrocities.

Arguing from the other side – Now you may loudly bicker from the other side of the fence about how you and such companies are providing employment to millions worldwide, which they would not have had if such businesses didn't exist. Agreed, it is generating tons of employment globally and has plenty of economic and lifestyle benefits for everyone. And it does not mean we should stop and switch off everything. But the issue here is about the intensity of slave labor and the herculean consumption of precious raw materials to meet the insatiable thirst for newer and newer products every day. The moderation in modernization is missing, and it will eventually blow up in your face. It is the difference between driving within speed limits and driving recklessly and accelerating like there is no tomorrow. If, as a demanding customer, you keep demanding a newer and cheaper model every three months, then there will be tough people who will step in to fulfill your need through hook or crook.

While such businesses do generate great employment, this kind of intense modern slavery is a recent phenomenon arising from unnecessary greed for owning a bunch of useless, non-biodegradable stuff just to look cool. Secondly, would you be gladly willing to send your child to work in a slave factory for 18 hours a day, getting a pittance, to satisfy the never-ending greed of the modern customer? Would your mother wholeheartedly allow you to work in a slave factory? I think not. The issue here is how you are continuously gaining sin points by directly or indirectly sponsoring crime through your greed for a never-ending supply of unnecessary stuff. You may now argue what those poor people will do without a job that you have so graciously created. Simple, if such businesses don't exist, then those poor people would continue to do what their forefathers did for centuries and centuries, like agriculture or simple mom-and-pop stores.

Secondly, trying to win arguments with the usual examples revolving around laws of economics, demand and supply, global competitiveness, shareholder value, and other financial statistical gymnastics does not make everything a righteous act. Sin is about listening to what your conscience and heart say, and not only about money adventures. Besides, as Lou Holtz says, if you burn your neighbor's house down, it doesn't make your house look any better."

"Hmm, but do I reduce my sins?"

"Simple, start asking yourself some hard questions about your lifestyle and the reckless consumerism you follow.

Question-1: What responsibility do you, as a customer, have in demanding an endless supply of useless gadgets and other cool things? Why do you need to change your phone every six months? Think of the direct and indirect costs to everyone.

Question-2: It is not the human cost alone that matters. What about the environmental costs? Today's demanding customers are also responsible for forests disappearing, rivers and oceans getting polluted, animals and birds dying, etc., in their relentless hunt for precious raw materials required to manufacture cool stuff. Explore some examples.

Example-1: Why do you need a gadget for anything and everything that continuously consumes electricity or batteries? Do you inquire about who makes the silly gadgets you use, the herculean human costs involved, the terrible environmental impact, or where the old useless gadgets disappear when the cool upgrade gets released every three months? And are you aware that whenever you visit a clean and pretty-smelling gadget store filled with tons of shiny, cool products, there is an ugly story or a slave factory behind it?

Example-2: Why do you need to change your car every two years? Is it necessary for a hundred different car and bike manufacturers worldwide to release dozens of new, mild and wild, gas-guzzling models every year by plundering the earth and oceans for iron, steel, and other raw materials required to manufacture them? Should you applaud them for churning out cars and bikes that can go from 0 to 200 mph in five seconds?

Example-3: Why do companies have to release some 50 different models of mobiles, 30 types of printers, 15 models of computers, and umpteen electronic gadgets every six months with teeny-weeny feature differences between them? Even popular models of many things are not allowed to last more than a few months by their manufacturers claiming to be under tremendous pressure to innovate and release something new. So, they keep on churning out newer and newer models by changing the shape, color, smell, design, etc. Remember, none of them will last even one or two years, as everything is designed for use and throw, and there is no reuse possibility to save the environment.

Question-3: Why is your home filled with mountains of useless stuff? Why does everyone in your family need two dozen shoes, one dozen watches, half a dozen goggles, three cars, etc.? When you say you are giving the best to your family, it only means you are raising spoiled brats who will also grow up chasing material wealth. This is how the world today is filled with weird, selfish, and spoilt children pampered by sissy parents who are unable and unwilling to teach them good values. And is it necessary for you to go on an expensive vacation twice a year, consuming jet fuel to eco-sensitive places and destroying forests, rivers, animals, etc., already inundated with a never-ending stream of ignorant tourists?

Question-4: Why do you ignore small mom-and-pop stores and buy everything from a large supermarket just for a little extra discount? Shouldn't your wealth be shared among the community and allow mom-and-pop stores to survive, and not make a rich conglomerate even richer?

Question-5: How about feeling a little guilty making a sack of money when the stock price jumps due to a glamorous downsizing and the ruining of your fellow humans? As an uncaring, demanding customer, how many mighty slave factories are you sponsoring? Do you know countless, helpless workers as young as ten years old are made to stand and work for long hours till their hands and legs swell up and they can hardly walk? What about the tears and pain of their mothers? Or are they all expendable as long as you get that cool gadget on time?

This is how the curses of thousands of mothers will hit you from countless directions. In other words, invisible bloodstains and tears are clinging to you. Today your shiny new gadgets, cars, reckless spending, your fancy lifestyle, and other stuff you own are the new blood diamonds!

"Now will you still confidently claim that you are no sinner?"

"You are amazing, professor. I had never thought of such things. Yes, we are all sinners, directly or indirectly."

The long conclusion - Curses are nature's harsh teachers created to ensure people live moderately. Nature punishes everyone for the mistakes of a few. And it does not matter whether humans believe in it or not. Refusing to believe does not make it a lie.

Nature does not require any human's belief or permission to activate its features. It is like a strict teacher punishing the entire class for controlling a few mischievous kids. Committing sins is like wallowing in the dirt (curse). If you are reckless and roll in the mud, then a lot of dirt will cling to you. But if you are moderate and restrained, then very little dirt will cling to you. The question is how much dirt you want on your conscience for the sake of material happiness.

Also, many people wrongly assume that if they commit a sin, then the punishment for it should happen quickly within hours or days. Since it does not happen quickly, they argue there is no such thing as sin or curses. But it does not work that way. Curses have no time limit and can hit back years later in uncanny ways. It is like a time bomb or a time traveler. Sometimes a curse will not directly hit the person committing the crime, but it will hit the children of that person decades later.

Sin need not always be looked at from a spiritual or religious angle. It can also simply be viewed as mistakes or errors committed knowingly or unknowingly. For example, even in our material world, if product manufacturers of cars, mobiles, etc., commit mistakes in their design, assembly, or service, then such products will suffer from defects and low quality, isn't it? This concept applies to humans also, as we are self-governing products created by nature. So, if parents commit sins, then their children have to suffer because children are the products created by their parents. This is why you see many children suffering for the misdeeds of their parents.

Similarly, innocent members of various human clans suffer from the atrocities committed by their guilty members. Descendants of barbarians suffer for centuries for the atrocities committed by their barbaric forefathers. Countries suffer for the sins committed by their reckless leaders and past citizens. The descendants of those who harassed someone will suffer from the descendants of those who suffered. Shareholders have to suffer for the sins committed by the companies they invest their money in. And without knowing all these hidden reasons, people ask tough questions like why good people suffer, why bad things happen to good people, etc. But it is actually a curse clinging to them for various known and unknown reasons.

But how does it actually work? - To understand the working of a curse in a different way, just understand that humans are basically energy bundles that can emit or absorb good or bad energies by doing something, or even when they are standing still. For example, when you hear a sound, you are absorbing energy through your ears, and when you are talking, you are emitting energy from your mouth. Similarly, when you are looking at something, the light energy is entering your eyes. Or if you are giving an inspiring speech, you can pump motivational energy into thousands of listeners. Or see examples of how a powerful stare can make another human uneasy, make him sick, or even make him commit horrific crimes, like how dictators have used their icy eye power on their subordinates.

Even your human thoughts, touch, and eyesight are all special forms of energy that cannot be detected or measured by any scientific instruments. This is why we have numerous examples of telepathy, hypnosis, or the special healing touch of many doctors, nurses, and healers that science cannot explain. Similarly, a curse is a special vengeful energy or an infectious disease that can cling to objects or people and cause havoc for many years. It is a justice system designed by nature and can get activated when you do bad things to others or vice versa. For example, even during your school or college days, if somebody copied your entire exam answers, you would definitely wish that student would fail or break a leg. Or if someone stole all your good ideas, patented them, and made tons of money, would you be happy? Or if someone killed your family members and stole their valuables, would you simply ignore it? In other words, you will put a curse on them because you wouldn't want those rascals to enjoy or benefit from it. And this curse of any sins can travel and exact revenge years later. That is how the law of sins and curses (or reap what you sow) works. You can run, but you can't hide!

Finally, remember one more thing. It is impossible to be fully sin-free, as we all commit various sins every day. And as you saw before, sin affects all of us, whether we commit sins ourselves or when we allow others to sin on our behalf. Secondly, you may not be able to make major global changes alone or overnight to reduce the swamp of sins all around, nor can you abruptly switch off your standard of living and head for the hills to live like a hermit. But gradually changing your lifestyle to a moderate level, controlling your kids from reckless consumerism, feeling guilty or repentant about many things you do, indulging in higher charity, and shedding some genuine tears for the sufferings of others will greatly reduce your sins. So, draw your boundaries even if you get laughed at. Learn to reject the high price of endless material growth to lead a rich and simple life.

I hope you now understand how many seemingly unrelated activities can make you a sinner, or why, despite earning more money than your parents, owning better gadgets, living in a luxurious house, having a superior standard of living, or pampering your kids, etc., you still don't have peace of mind. Now, do you agree with those ignorant, foolish, silly, brainless, irrational, crazy, and ridiculous spiritual believers you always loved to laugh at? But it is still not too late to change. However, if this goes on, Mother Nature may soon lose her patience and erupt like,

"All right! But hear me, and hear me well. The day will come. Oh yes, mark my words – Greedy Humans. Your day of reckoning is coming. When an evil wind will blow through your little playfield and wipe that

smug smile off your face. And I will be there, in all my glory, watching – watching as it all comes crumbling down!"

(A quote from Seinfeld, a popular TV sitcom)

Other Books by the Author

Personal Planner

Personal Disaster Preparedness Planner

Organize your Information, Belongings, and
Activities to Protect your Family in a Crisis

Humor Books

Become a Dictator
A Short and Snappy Guide

Become a Modern Artist
The Greatest and Easiest Job on Earth

Big Money
Top Secret Guide to the Stock Market Circus

The Mirage Peddlers
How to Become an Advertising Guru

The Mud Horse
Fantastic Jobs for Firebrand Feminists

Spirituality Books

The Miracle Law
The Pristine Path to Purpose and Prosperity

The Inventor of Nothing
A Mild and Wild Chat with the Brilliant Cosmic Designer

Personal Development Books

The Power of Laziness
Discovering the Wisdom of Slowness

The Extreme Minimalist
Discovering the Joys of Minimalism and Frugality

Get to the Point
A Short and Snappy Guide

The Curses of a Thousand Mothers
How We Pursue Joyful Sins

The Long Fuse
Why the Buddha Never Took Aspirin

No Easy Future!
Seven Habits to Tackle Tomorrow

The Compass Mind
A Short Guide to Think in All Directions

Start Saying NO!
How to Stop Living for Others and Start
Pursuing your Goals

The Gibraltar Briefcase
The Wise Weapons of Exceptional Executives

The Glass Prison
The How to Stay Productive during a
Lockdown

Children Books

Secret Trip to a Jolly Jungle
The Adventures of Tommy and his Magic
Spaceship

Secret Trip into the Ocean
The Adventures of Tommy and his Magic
Spaceship

Secret Trip to a Treasure Island
The Adventures of Tommy and his Magic
Spaceship

Secret Trip to Outer Space
The Adventures of Tommy and his Magic
Spaceship

The Magic Apple and his Mighty Friends

Technology Books

IT Asset Management
A Practical Guide for Technical and Business Executives

Disaster Recovery and Business Continuity
A Quick Guide for Organizations and Business Managers

Practical IT Service Management
A Concise Guide for Busy Executives

Fiction Books

FINK!
The Mafia's Nightmare

The Patriot's Confession
A Spy Thriller

The World's Shortest Novels
The Sixty Seconds Bookshelf

Personal Development Magazine
Wealth of the Wise

All the above books are available in both Paperback and eBook on all major book retailers

Author Services

Become an Author Course - Do you dream of becoming an Author? Do you want to share your Knowledge, Imagination, or Experience and write your first Fiction or Non-Fiction Book? Then take my Self-Paced Video Course on Thinkific for just US$79.95. The link is below.

https://thejendra.thinkific.com/courses/how-to-become-an-author-and-self-publish-your-book

Publish your Book Project - If you have already written a book and want to publish it, then I can help you to Self-Publish it Worldwide on all major book retailers in both Paperback and all eBook formats through my unique Assisted Self Publishing method.

Visit http://www.author-world.com for details

About the Author

Good day. My name is **Thejendra Sreenivas**. I was a Technology Manager in the IT industry for nearly 30 years. Before entering the IT industry, I was also an electronics lecturer for a short duration.

I have written and self-published 35+ books on various subjects. All my books are available in both Paperback and eBook on all major book retailers. I am also the Editor and Publisher of a font-optimized digital magazine called **Personal Development Magazine** which contains articles on personal development, workplace issues, humor, writing, and publishing.

I am now a **Book Publishing Coach** and offer services like *Assisted Self-Publishing, Manuscript Formatting, Facebook Ads, Ghostwriting, One Page Websites, Article Writing, and Podcast Creation.* In addition, I also offer Personal Development Coaching.

Please visit my web cave - **www.thejendra.com** or **www.author-world.com** for details of my books, magazine, and coaching information.

www.ingramcontent.com/pod-product-compliance
Lightning Source LLC
Chambersburg PA
CBHW021939170526
45157CB00005B/2352